M000011371

LABORATORY MANUAL TO ACCOMPANY

Security Policies and Implementation Issues

VERSION 2.0

Powered by vLab Solutions

JONES & BARTLETT
LEARNING

World Headquarters
Jones & Bartlett Learning
5 Wall Street
Burlington, MA 01803
978-443-5000
info@jblearning.com
www.jblearning.com

Jones & Bartlett Learning books and products are available through most bookstores and online booksellers. To contact Jones & Bartlett Learning directly, call 800-832-0034, fax 978-443-8000, or visit our website, www.jblearning.com.

Substantial discounts on bulk quantities of Jones & Bartlett Learning publications are available to corporations, professional associations, and other qualified organizations. For details and specific discount information, contact the special sales department at Jones & Bartlett Learning via the above contact information or send an email to specialsales@jblearning.com.

Production Credits

Chief Executive Officer: Ty Field
President: James Homer
Chief Product Officer: Eduardo Moura
SVP, Curriculum Solutions: Christopher Will
Director of Sales, Curriculum Solutions: Randi Roger
Author: vLab Solutions, LLC, David Kim, President
Editorial Management: High Stakes Writing, LLC,
  Lawrence J. Goodrich, President
Copy Editor, High Stakes Writing: Katherine Dillin
Developmental Editor, High Stakes Writing: Dee
  Hayes

Associate Program Manager: Rainna Erikson
Production Manager: Susan Beckett
Rights & Photo Research Associate: Lauren Miller
Manufacturing and Inventory Control Supervisor:
  Amy Bacus
Senior Marketing Manager: Andrea DeFronzo
Cover Design: Scott Moden
Cover Image: © HunThomas/ShutterStock, Inc.
Printing and Binding: Edwards Brothers Malloy
Cover Printing: Edwards Brothers Malloy

ISBN: 978-1-284-05916-8

6048

Printed in the United States of America

18 17 16 15 14   10 9 8 7 6 5 4 3 2 1

Contents

iv

Ethics and Your Personal Responsibilities

The material presented in this course is designed to give you a real-life look at the use of various tools and systems that are at the heart of every cybersecurity practitioner's daily responsibilities. During this course, you will have access to software and techniques used by professionals to investigate and test the security of critical infrastructures and information technology systems and devices. With this access come certain ethical responsibilities:

1. Do not exceed your authorized level of access. This includes remaining within your authorized level of access when using lab-provided software tools to scan or attack computers and software applications as directed within the lab procedures.

2. Do not attempt to use your authorized access for unauthorized purposes either inside or outside of the VSCL environment.

3. Do not attempt to attack or otherwise compromise the confidentiality, integrity, or availability of *any* IT systems, services, or infrastructures outside of the VSCL.

4. Comply with your academic institution's *Code of Student Conduct* and all other applicable policies and regulations.

5. Comply with applicable federal, state, and local laws regarding the use and misuse of information technology systems and services.

6. Comply with applicable laws regarding intellectual property rights, including patents and trademarks and copyrights.

Preface

Welcome! This lab manual is your step-by-step guide to completing the laboratory exercises for this course. You will have an opportunity to gain valuable hands-on experience with professional-grade tools and techniques as you work through the lab activities and answer the lab questions found at the end of each lab.

How to Use This Lab Manual

This lab manual features step-by-step instructions for completing the following hands-on lab exercises:

Lab #	Lab Title
1	Crafting an Organization-Wide Security Management Policy for Acceptable Use
2	Developing an Organization-Wide Policy Framework Implementation Plan
3	Defining an Information Systems Security Policy Framework for an IT Infrastructure
4	Crafting a Layered Security Management Policy—Separation of Duties
5	Crafting an Organization-Wide Security Awareness Training Policy
6	Defining a Remote Access Policy to Support Remote Health Care Clinics
7	Identifying Necessary Policies for Business Continuity—BIA and Recovery Time Objectives
8	Crafting a Security or Computer Incident Response Policy—CIRT Response Team
9	Assessing and Auditing an Existing IT Security Policy Framework Definition
10	Aligning an IT Security Policy Framework to the Seven Domains of a Typical IT Infrastructure

Step-by-Step Instructions

For each lab, you are provided with detailed, step-by-step instructions and screen captures showing the results of key steps within the lab. All actions that you are required to take are shown in **bold** font. The screen captures will also help you identify menus, dialog boxes, and input locations.

Deliverables

As you work through each lab, you will be instructed to record specific information or take a screen capture to document the results you obtained by performing specific actions. The deliverables are designed to test your understanding of the information, and your successful completion of the steps and functions of the lab. All of these documentation tasks should be pasted into a single file (MS Word .doc, .docx, or other compatible format) and submitted for grading by your instructor.

You will create two deliverable files for each lab:

- *Lab Report file* (including screen captures taken at specific steps in the lab)
- *Lab Assessment file* (including answers to questions posed at the end of each lab)

You may use either Microsoft® Word or any other compatible word processing software for these deliverables. For specific information on deliverables, refer to the Deliverables section in each lab.

Lab Assessment File

At the end of each lab, there is a set of questions which are to be answered and submitted for grading in the Lab Assessment file. (Your instructor may provide alternate instructions for this deliverable.) For some questions, you may need to refer to your Lab Report file to obtain information from the lab. For other questions, you may need to consult a textbook or other authoritative source to obtain more information.

Web References

URLs for Web resources listed in this laboratory manual are subject to change without prior notice. These links were last verified on April 26, 2014. Many times, you can find the required resource by using an Internet search engine and a partial URL or keywords. You may also search the Internet Archives (also referred to as the "Wayback Machine") for a given URL that is no longer available at the original Web site (http://www.archive.org).

Technical Support

If you need help completing a lab in this manual, contact the Jones & Bartlett Learning Help Desk using the information below. Remember to include the name of your institution and reference the course name and number in your ticket details

Phone: 1-866-601-4525

Online: http://www.jblcourses.com/techsupport

Monday-Thursday:	8AM – 10PM
Friday:	8AM – 8PM
Saturday:	8AM – 5PM
Sunday:	10AM – 11PM
(All hours are EST)	

If you need help outside of these hours, submit an online ticket or leave a message on our toll-free phone line, and someone from the help desk will get back to you as soon as possible.

Credits

Adobe Reader® is a registered trademark of Adobe Systems Incorporated in the United States and/or other countries. Active Directory®, Excel®, Microsoft®, Windows®, and Windows Server® are registered trademarks of Microsoft Corporation in the United States and/or other countries. Linux® is a registered trademark of Linus Torvalds. Citrix® is a registered trademark of Citrix Systems, Inc. and/or one or more of its subsidiaries, and may be registered in the United States Patent and Trademark Office and in other countries. FileZilla® is a registered trademark of Tim Kosse. Firefox® is a registered trademark of the Mozilla Foundation. Nessus® is a registered trademark of Tenable Network Security. NetWitness® is a registered trademark of EMC Corporation in the United States and other countries. Nmap Security Scanner® and Zenmap® are either registered trademarks or trademarks of Insecure.com LLC. Wireshark® is a registered trademark of the Wireshark Foundation. pfSense® is a federally registered trademark of Electric Sheep Fencing LLC. Debian® is a registered trademark of Software in the Public Interest, Inc. Retina® is a registered trademark of BeyondTrust, Inc. Openswan® is an unregistered trademark of Xelerance.

All brand names and product names used in this document are trademarks, registered trademarks, or trade names of their respective holders.

Lab #1 Crafting an Organization-Wide Security Management Policy for Acceptable Use

Introduction

When given access to resources, whether IT equipment or some other type of asset, most people will use the resources responsibly. However, a few people, when left to rely on only common courtesy or good judgment, will misuse or abuse those resources. The misuse might be for their own benefit or just for entertainment. While the misuse can be unintentional, it is still a waste of resources. To avoid that waste or outright abuse, a company will document official guidance. For resources within the IT domains, that guidance is called an acceptable use policy (AUP).

An AUP's purpose is to establish the rules for a specific system, network, or Web site. These policies outline the rules for achieving compliance, for example. They also help an organization mitigate risks and threats because they establish what can and cannot take place.

In this lab, you will define an AUP as it relates to the User Domain, you will identify the key elements of sample AUPs, you will learn how to mitigate threats and risks with an AUP, and you will create your own AUP for an organization.

Learning Objectives

Upon completing this lab, you will be able to:

- Define the scope of an acceptable use policy (AUP) as it relates to the User Domain.
- Identify the key elements of acceptable use in an organization's overall security management framework.
- Align an AUP with the organization's goals for compliance.
- Mitigate the common risks and threats caused by users in the User Domain with the implementation of an AUP.
- Draft an AUP in accordance with the policy framework definition that incorporates a policy statement, standards, procedures, and guidelines.

Deliverables

Upon completion of this lab, you are required to provide the following deliverables to your instructor:

1. Lab Report file;
2. Lab Assessments file.

Hands-On Steps

> ▶**Note:**
> This is a paper-based lab. To successfully complete the deliverables for this lab, you will need access to Microsoft® Word or another compatible word processor. For some labs, you may also need access to a graphics line drawing application, such as Visio or PowerPoint. Refer to the Preface of this manual for information on creating the lab deliverable files.

1. On your local computer, **create** the **lab deliverable files**.

2. **Review** the **Lab Assessment Worksheet**. You will find answers to these questions as you proceed through the lab steps.

3. Using Figure 1, **review** the seven domains of a typical IT infrastructure.

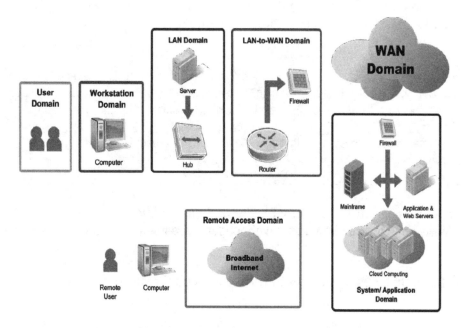

Figure 1 Seven domains of a typical IT infrastructure

4. On your local computer, **open** a new **Internet browser window**.

5. In the address box of your Internet browser, **type** the URL **http://cve.mitre.org** and **press Enter** to open the Web site.

> **▶Note:**
> CVE stands for Common Vulnerabilities and Exposures, which is a reference system originated by the MITRE Corporation for cataloging known information security vulnerabilities. While MITRE is a U.S. not-for-profit organization, the U.S. Department of Homeland Security provides a portion of the funding to support the CVE database.

6. On the Web site's left side, **click** the **Search CVE link**.

7. In the box on the right titled CVE List Master Copy, **click View CVE List**.

8. In the Search Master Copy of CVE box at the bottom of the page, **type User Domain** into the **By Keyword(s)** area and **click Submit**.

9. **Search** the resulting list of articles for entries related to the User Domain.

10. In your Lab Report file, **identify** the risks, threats, and vulnerabilities commonly found in the User Domain. (**Name** at least **three** risks/threats.)

> **▶Note:**
> Your search for relevant risks will be difficult due to the high number of vulnerabilities related to Windows® Active Directory® domains, as opposed to the "User Domain" as one of the seven IT asset domains. Try additional words that describe user-particular risks or threats, for example, surfing, phishing, malicious, downloads, etc.
>
> Consider listed vulnerabilities, such as those that allow an authenticated user to gain unauthorized privileges, or steal others' passwords or files.

11. In the address box of your Internet browser, **type** the URL **http://www.sans.org/reading_room/whitepapers/threats/** and **press Enter** to open the Web site.

12. **Scroll** through the list of articles to find articles on threats and vulnerabilities in the User Domain.

13. **Choose** two articles that discuss two of the risks or threats you listed in step 10.

14. In your Lab Report file, **discuss** how these articles explain how to mitigate risks or threats in the User Domain.

15. In the address box of your Internet browser, **type** the following URLs and **press Enter** to open the Web sites:

   - Health care: **http://it.jhu.edu/policies/itpolicies.html**
   - Higher education: **http://www.brown.edu/information-technology/computing-policies/acceptable-use-policy**
   - U.S. federal government: **https://www.jointservicessupport.org/AUP.aspx**

16. In your Lab Report file, **list** the main components of each of the acceptable use policies (AUPs) documented at each of these sites.

17. In your Lab Report file, **explain** how a risk can be mitigated in the User Domain with an acceptable use policy (AUP). Base your answer on what you discovered in the previous step.

18. **Consider** the following fictional organization, which needs an acceptable use policy (AUP):

- The organization is a regional XYZ Credit Union/Bank that has multiple branches and locations throughout the region.
- Online banking and use of the Internet are the bank's strengths, given its limited human resources.
- The customer service department is the organization's most critical business function.
- The organization wants to be in compliance with the Gramm-Leach-Bliley Act (GLBA) and IT security best practices regarding its employees.
- The organization wants to monitor and control use of the Internet by implementing content filtering.
- The organization wants to eliminate personal use of organization-owned IT assets and systems.
- The organization wants to monitor and control use of the e-mail system by implementing e-mail security controls.
- The organization wants to implement this policy for all the IT assets it owns and to incorporate this policy review into its annual security awareness training.

> ▶**Note:**
> The best style for writing IT policy is straightforward and easy to understand. Avoid "fluff," or unnecessary wording, and phrasing that could be understood more than one way. Write in concise, direct language.

19. Using the following AUP template, in your Lab Report file, **create** an acceptable use policy for the XYZ Credit Union/Bank organization (this should not be longer than three pages):

XYZ Credit Union/Bank

Policy Name

Policy Statement

{Insert policy verbiage here.}

Purpose/Objectives

{Insert the policy's purpose as well as its objectives; include a bulleted list of the policy definition.}

Scope

{Define this policy's scope and whom it covers.

Which of the seven domains of a typical IT infrastructure are impacted?

What elements, IT assets, or organization-owned assets are within this policy's scope?}

Standards

{Does this policy point to any hardware, software, or configuration standards? If so, list them here and explain the relationship of this policy to these standards.}

Procedures

{In this section, explain how you intend to implement this policy throughout this organization.}

Guidelines

{In this section, explain any roadblocks or implementation issues that you must overcome and how you will overcome them per the defined policy guidelines.}

▶ **Note:**
This completes the lab. **Close** the **Web browser**, if you have not already done so.

Evaluation Criteria and Rubrics

The following are the evaluation criteria for this lab that students must perform:

1. Define the scope of an acceptable use policy (AUP) as it relates to the User Domain. – **[20%]**
2. Identify the key elements of acceptable use in an organization's overall security management framework. – **[20%]**
3. Align an AUP with the organization's goals for compliance. – **[20%]**
4. Mitigate the common risks and threats caused by users in the User Domain with the implementation of an AUP. – **[20%]**
5. Draft an AUP in accordance with the policy framework definition that incorporates a policy statement, standards, procedures, and guidelines. – **[20%]**

Lab #1 - Assessment Worksheet

Crafting an Organization-Wide Security Management Policy for Acceptable Use

Course Name and Number: _____

Student Name: _____

Instructor Name: _____

Lab Due Date: _____

Overview

In this lab, you defined an AUP as it relates to the User Domain, you identified the key elements of sample AUPs, you learned how to mitigate threats and risks with an AUP, and you created your own AUP for an organization.

Lab Assessment Questions & Answers

1. What are three risks and threats of the User Domain?

2. Why do organizations have acceptable use policies (AUPs)?

3. Can Internet use and e-mail use policies be covered in an acceptable use policy?

4. Do compliance laws, such as the Health Insurance Portability and Accountability Act (HIPAA) or GLBA, play a role in AUP definition?

5. Why is an acceptable use policy not a fail-safe means of mitigating risks and threats within the User Domain?

6. Will the AUP apply to all levels of the organization? Why or why not?

7. When should an AUP be implemented and how?

8. Why would an organization want to align its policies with existing compliance requirements?

9. In which domain of the seven domains of a typical IT infrastructure would an acceptable use policy (AUP) reside? How does an AUP help mitigate the risks commonly found with employees and authorized users of an organization's IT infrastructure?

10. Why must an organization have an acceptable use policy (AUP) even for nonemployees, such as contractors, consultants, and other third parties?

11. What security controls can be deployed to monitor and mitigate users from accessing external Web sites that are potentially in violation of an AUP?

12. What security controls can be deployed to monitor and mitigate users from accessing external webmail systems and services (for example, Hotmail®, Gmail™, Yahoo!®, etc.)?

13. Should an organization terminate the employment of an employee if he/she violates an AUP?

Lab #2 Developing an Organization-Wide Policy Framework Implementation Plan

Introduction

Employees are people, not machines. Consequently, employee behavior is far from optimal and is instead prone to create insecure work environments. This is why organizations create policies and offer guidance. This guidance comes from initiatives such as security awareness training.

Employee attitudes toward security awareness training can range from indifferent to eager. Naturally, an employee's willingness to work and learn is subjective, but most relevant here is the employee's adherence to information security policy. To ensure employees aren't apathetic about security policy can depend on a number of factors, including organization structure. For example, an organization's structure may be hierarchical or flat. Which one it is will generally determine a predictable pattern of employee behavior. But regardless of whether an organization is hierarchical or flat, you can create an organizational policy framework to define policies that mitigate risks and threats.

In this lab, you will identify human nature and behaviors in hierarchical and flat organizations, you will find ways to ensure employees overcome apathy related to security awareness, you will identify how security policies shape organizational behaviors and culture, you will compare hierarchical and flat organizational structures, and you will create an organizational policy implementation plan for a combined organizational structure.

Learning Objectives

Upon completing this lab, you will be able to:

- Identify human nature and behavior patterns of employee types in both hierarchical and flat organizational structures.
- Overcome user apathy with security awareness techniques in both hierarchical and flat organizational structures.
- Identify how security policies can help shape organizational behavior and culture in both hierarchical and flat organizational structures.
- Compare a hierarchical and a flat organizational structure with equivalent IT security policy framework structures.
- Create an organizational policy implementation plan for a combined organizational structure.

Deliverables

Upon completion of this lab, you are required to provide the following deliverables to your instructor:

1. Lab Report file;
2. Lab Assessments file.

Hands-On Steps

> ▶**Note:**
> This is a paper-based lab. To successfully complete the deliverables for this lab, you will need access to Microsoft® Word or another compatible word processor. For some labs, you may also need access to a graphics line drawing application, such as Visio or PowerPoint. Refer to the Preface of this manual for information on creating the lab deliverable files.

1. On your local computer, **create** the **lab deliverable files**.

2. **Review** the **Lab Assessment Worksheet**. You will find answers to these questions as you proceed through the lab steps.

3. **Review** the following information about executive management, IT security policy enforcement monitoring, and human resources, all of which must have a unified front regarding disciplinary treatment of policy violations:

   - **Executive Management:** Policy commitment and implementation must come from the chief executive officer (CEO) and the president's executive order for the entire organization with policy monitoring and disciplinary action taken for policy violations.
   - **IT Security Policy Enforcement Monitoring:** Policy monitoring can be conducted via system logging, content filtering logging, and e-mail filtering logging with automated reporting to IT security personnel for monthly or quarterly policy compliance reviews.
   - **Human Resources:** Employees, contractors, and consultants must conform to all organization-wide policies. Violations of policies are considered to be an employer-employee issue upon which proper disciplinary actions must be taken. Repeat or continued violations of organization-wide policies might be grounds for termination of employment, depending on the violation's severity. Nonemployees should be provided with limited access and connectivity as per policy definition.

4. **Review** the following information about the organizational structure inherent in flat and hierarchical organizations and how people behave in these structures:

   - **Flat organizational structures are characterized by the following:**
     o The management structure is cross-functional and more open to employee input.
     o Dialogue and communications between employees can occur across organizational functions.
     o Employees tend to be more open and communicative.
     o Employees tend to be more creative and involved in business decisions.
     o Employees are not as constrained within their role or function and can see and interact across the organization more freely.

- **Hierarchical organizational structures are characterized by the following:**
  - Departments are separated by function, creating multiple functional silos.
  - Business decision making is performed at the executive management level.
  - Dialogue and communications are more "top-down."
  - Employees tend to be less communicative and more isolated within their business functions.
  - Employees find it difficult to offer additional creativity or input to business decisions.
  - Employees are constrained within their roles and cannot interact outside of their business functions without going through a chain of command.

5. On your local computer, **open** a new **Internet browser window.**

6. In the address box of your Internet browser, **type** the URL http://www.ehow.com/info_11369248_employees--behave-differently-flat-vs-hierarchical-organizational-structure.html and **press Enter** to open the Web site.

7. **Read** this article about how employees behave differently in contrasting organizations.

8. In your Lab Report file, **discuss** how employee behavior changes depending on the organizational structure in which the employee works.

> ▶**Note:**
> To highlight something briefly mentioned in the eHow article, a prominent difference between companies with hierarchical and flat structures is size. A company's size can affect employee behavior as much as the structure or other factors can, especially an employee's sense of job security, purpose, and potential to contribute to the company's whole success. These factors can make an employee feel dissatisfied or even apathetic.

9. **Review** the following information about why conducting annual audits and security assessments for policy compliance are critical security operations and management functions that can help mitigate risks and threats:

   - People constantly change (they grow on the job, move to new jobs, etc.).
   - People gravitate toward repetition and repetitive inputs.
   - Periodic security awareness training coupled with policy compliance monitoring can help mitigate the risks and threats caused by employees.

10. In your Lab Report file, **create** a policy framework implementation plan for the fictional Specialty Medical Clinic (the plan should not be longer than three pages). The Specialty Medical Clinic is being acquired by a larger parent organization under the Health Insurance Portability and Accountability Act (HIPAA) compliance law. The parent organization is a hierarchical structure with multiple departments and clinics. The medical clinic is a flat organization. Following is an outline of those areas of the plan you need to include:

Parent Medical Clinic

Acquires Specialty Medical Clinic

Publish Your Policies for the New Clinic

{Explain your strategy.}

Communicate Your Policies to the New Clinic Employees

{How are you going to do this?}

> ▶ **Note:**
> Special all-hands meetings called "Town Hall meetings" can be held between team or departmental leads. Team leaders might then share the information they've gained from Town Hall meetings with employees.

Involve Human Resources and Executive Management

{How do you do this smoothly?}

Incorporate Security Awareness and Training for the New Clinic

{How can you make this fun and engaging?}

Security Awareness Training How-To

Employees typically dread mandatory security awareness training. It can be dry, not relevant to their positions, and a distraction from what they're paid to do. It doesn't have to be, though.

As with any training, security awareness training can be more effective if made unconventional or interactive. For example, if instead of an employee simply reading policy and then taking an assessment quiz, the employee could participate in a role-playing exercise with teams of "good guys" and "bad guys." This takes considerably more planning, but once designed for a small group, the exercise is easily repeatable. The training will likely be talked about and remembered for much longer.

User behavior will also more likely be changed if the training is tailored to the employee and his or her specific department. An employee in shipping will be more receptive if security topics are in context of the freight docks rather than mostly relevant to a cubicle setting. Relevance counts a lot toward actual learning.

Lastly, the rationale behind the security training must be explained. Without presenting the "why" or the consequences, the employee has little reason to internalize the valuable training.

Release a Monthly Organization-Wide Newsletter for All

{How can you make this newsletter succinct?}

Implement Security Reminders on System Logon Screens for All

{This is for access to sensitive systems only.}

Incorporate Ongoing Security Policy Maintenance for All

{Review and obtain feedback from employees and policy-compliance monitoring.}

> ▶ **Note:**
> Be mindful that a new policy or procedure doesn't negatively impact a business process or create unintended challenges in a particular department. When users find that a policy is going to make their jobs harder, they're much more likely to try to circumvent that policy.
>
> Employee feedback may be the only method for revealing how a policy might impose unintended challenges on an employee. Be certain to clearly communicate, to leaders and employees alike, that feedback must be open, honest, and may be given without any fear of adverse repercussions.

Obtain Employee Questions or Feedback for Policy Board

{Review and incorporate into policy edits and changes as needed.}

> ▶ **Note:**
> This completes the lab. **Close** the **Web browser**, if you have not already done so.

Evaluation Criteria and Rubrics

The following are the evaluation criteria for this lab that students must perform:

1. Identify human nature and behavior patterns of employee types in both hierarchical and flat organizational structures. – **[20%]**
2. Overcome user apathy with security awareness techniques in both hierarchical and flat organizational structures. – **[20%]**
3. Identify how security policies can help shape organizational behavior and culture in both hierarchical and flat organizational structures. – **[20%]**
4. Compare a hierarchical and a flat organizational structure with equivalent IT security policy framework structures. – **[20%]**
5. Create an organizational policy implementation plan for a combined organizational structure. – **[20%]**

Lab #2 - Assessment Worksheet

Developing an Organization-Wide Policy Framework Implementation Plan

Course Name and Number: _____

Student Name: _____

Instructor Name: _____

Lab Due Date: _____

Overview

In this lab, you identified human nature and behaviors in hierarchical and flat organizations, you found ways to ensure employees overcome apathy related to security awareness, you identified how security policies shape organizational behaviors and culture, you compared hierarchical and flat organizational structures, and you created an organizational policy implementation plan for a combined organizational structure.

Lab Assessment Questions & Answers

1. What are the differences between flat and hierarchical organizations?

2. Do employees behave differently in a flat versus a hierarchical organizational structure? Explain your answer.

3. Do employee personality types differ between hierarchical and flat organizations?

4. What is difficult about policy implementation in a flat organization?

5. What is difficult about policy implementation in a hierarchical organization?

6. How do you overcome employee apathy toward policy compliance?

Lab #3 Defining an Information Systems Security Policy Framework for an IT Infrastructure

Introduction

In any company, a security policy helps to mitigate the risks and threats the business encounters. However, unless a company happens to be in the information security industry, the task of identifying, assessing, and categorizing the myriad of risks can be an overwhelming one. Thankfully, a company's IT infrastructure can be divided in a logical manner to more easily sort the risks. These divisions are the seven IT domains.

The purpose of the seven domains of a typical IT infrastructure is to help organize the roles, responsibilities, and accountabilities for risk management and risk mitigation.

In this lab, you will identify known risks, threats, and vulnerabilities, and you will determine which domain of a typical IT infrastructure is affected. You will then discuss security policies to address each identified risk and threat within the seven domains of a typical IT infrastructure. You will next determine which appropriate security policy definition will help mitigate the identified risk, threat, or vulnerability. You will organize your results into a framework that can become part of a layered security strategy.

Learning Objectives

Upon completing this lab, you will be able to:

- Identify risks, threats, and vulnerabilities commonly found in the seven domains of a typical IT infrastructure.
- Determine which domain is impacted by the risk, threat, or vulnerability.
- Determine security policies to address each identified risk and threat within the seven domains of a typical IT infrastructure.
- Select the appropriate policy definitions needed throughout the seven domains of a typical IT infrastructure to mitigate the identified risks, threats, and vulnerabilities.
- Organize the security policies in an overall framework as part of a layered security strategy for the seven domains of a typical IT infrastructure.

Deliverables

Upon completion of this lab, you are required to provide the following deliverables to your instructor:

1. Lab Report file;
2. Lab Assessments file.

Hands-On Steps

1. On your local computer, **create** the **lab deliverable files**.

2. **Review** the **Lab Assessment Worksheet**. You will find answers to these questions as you
   proceed through the lab steps.

3. **Review** the seven domains of a typical IT infrastructure (see Figure 1).

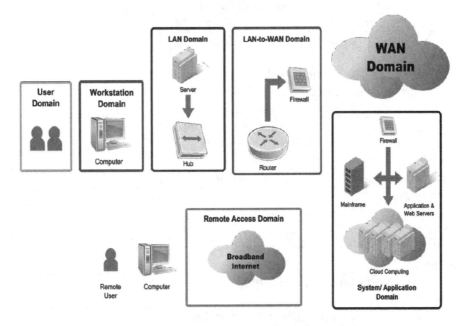

Figure 1 Seven domains of a typical IT infrastructure

4. On your local computer, **open** a new **Internet browser window**.

5. In the address box of your Internet browser, **type** the URL
   http://www.continuitycompliance.org/security-policy-components-of-a-good-policy/ and
   press Enter to open the Web site.

6. **Review** the information to determine the components of an information systems security
   policy.

7. In your Lab Report file, **identify** the major components of an information systems security policy.

8. **Review** the following table of risks, threats, and vulnerabilities that were found in a health care IT infrastructure servicing patients with life-threatening conditions:

Risks, Threats, and Vulnerabilities	Domain
Unauthorized access from public Internet	
Hacker penetrates IT infrastructure	
Communication circuit outages	
Workstation operating system (OS) has a known software vulnerability	
Unauthorized access to organization-owned data	
Denial of service attack on organization's e-mail	
Remote communications from home office	
Workstation browser has software vulnerability	
Weak ingress/egress traffic-filtering degrades performance	
Wireless Local Area Network (WLAN) access points are needed for Local Area Network (LAN) connectivity within a warehouse	
User destroys data in application, deletes all files, and gains access to internal network	
Fire destroys primary data center	
Intraoffice employee romance gone bad	
Loss of production data	
Need to prevent rogue users from unauthorized WLAN access	
LAN server OS has a known software vulnerability	
User downloads an unknown e-mail attachment	
Service provider has a major network outage	
User inserts CDs and USB hard drives with personal photos, music, and videos on organization-owned computers	
Virtual Private Network (VPN) tunneling between the remote computer and ingress/egress router	

9. In your Lab Report file, **align** each of the risks, threats, and vulnerabilities identified in the previous table to the domain impacted (refer to Figure 1 for the seven IT domains).

10. In your Lab Report file, **explain** how risks like these can be mitigated with an information systems security policy.

11. In the address box of your Internet browser, **type** the URL **http://www.sans.org/security-resources/policies/Policy_Primer.pdf** and **press Enter** to open the Web site.

12. **Read** the SANS Institute's document, "A Short Primer for Developing Security Policies."

13. In your Lab Report file, **define** what a policy is according to the SANS Institute.

> ▶**Note:**
> It is important to understand how and why a policy differs from a standard, a procedure, and a guideline. From the top down, the policy should not change or need modification unless a major shift in corporate values or business process occurs. On the contrary, guidelines should be reviewed, and possibly changed, often.
>
> Similarly, even though a policy should be written clearly and concisely, it is a high-level document answering the "why" questions. Standards are also high-level, but instead should answer the "what" questions. Finally, the procedures and guidelines provide the "how."

14. Using the SANS primer, in your Lab Report file, **describe** the basic requirements of policies, their benefits, the control factors, and policies every organization needs.

15. **Review** the identified risks, threats, and vulnerabilities in the table in step 8, and then **select** an appropriate policy definition that might help mitigate each of them. You can select one of the SANS policies or choose one from the following list:

Policy Definition List

- Acceptable Use Policy
- Access Control Policy Definition
- Business Continuity—Business Impact Analysis (BIA) Policy Definition
- Business Continuity & Disaster Recovery Policy Definition
- Data Classification Standard & Encryption Policy Definition
- Internet Ingress/Egress Traffic Policy Definition
- Mandated Security Awareness Training Policy Definition
- Production Data Backup Policy Definition
- Remote Access Policy Definition
- Vulnerability Management & Vulnerability Window Policy Definition
- Wide Area Network (WAN) Service Availability Policy Definition

16. In your Lab Report file, **organize** your security policies and the definitions you selected so that they can be used as part of an overall framework for a layered security strategy.

> ▶**Note:**
> This completes the lab. **Close** the **Web browser**, if you have not already done so.

Evaluation Criteria and Rubrics

The following are the evaluation criteria for this lab that students must perform:

1. Identify risks, threats, and vulnerabilities commonly found in the seven domains of a typical IT infrastructure. – **[20%]**
2. Determine which domain is impacted by the risk, threat, or vulnerability. – **[20%]**
3. Determine security policies to address each identified risk and threat within the seven domains of a typical IT infrastructure. – **[20%]**
4. Select the appropriate policy definitions needed throughout the seven domains of a typical IT infrastructure to mitigate the identified risks, threats, and vulnerabilities. – **[20%]**
5. Organize the security policies in an overall framework as part of a layered security strategy for the seven domains of a typical IT infrastructure. – **[20%]**

Lab #3 - Assessment Worksheet

Defining an Information Systems Security Policy Framework for an IT Infrastructure

Course Name and Number: _____

Student Name: _____

Instructor Name: _____

Lab Due Date: _____

Overview

In this lab, you identified known risks, threats, and vulnerabilities, and you determined which domain of a typical IT infrastructure was affected. You then discussed security policies to address each identified risk and threat within the seven domains of a typical IT infrastructure. You next determined which appropriate security policy definition helped mitigate the identified risk, threat, or vulnerability. You organized your results into a framework that could become part of a layered security strategy.

Lab Assessment Questions & Answers

1. What is the purpose of defining a framework for IT security policies?

2. What are the major components of an information systems security policy?

3. What is the definition of a policy?

4. What are the benefits of a policy?

5. What policy definition in the SANS primer or in the list provided in the lab is required to restrict and prevent unauthorized access to organization-owned IT systems and applications?

6. What policy definition in the SANS primer or in the list provided in the lab can help remind employees in the User Domain about ongoing acceptable use and unacceptable use?

7. Why should an organization have a remote access policy even if it already has an acceptable use policy (AUP) for employees?

8. What security controls can be implemented on your e-mail system to help prevent rogue or malicious software disguised as URL links or e-mail attachments from attacking the Workstation Domain? What kind of policy definition should you use?

9. Why should an organization have annual security awareness training that includes an overview of the organization's policies?

Lab #4 Crafting a Layered Security Management Policy—Separation of Duties

Introduction

Every job comes with its own particular set of duties and responsibilities. Businesses grant their employees the authority to carry out their work. Occasionally, though, an employee's duties may seem to conflict. For example, an employee's job may include "hardening" the servers. But then that same employee is asked to audit those very same servers for compliance. In a best case scenario, when that employee catches a compliance gap, he or she reports the gap in the audit. Unfortunately, the more likely scenario is, after the employee identifies the security gap, he or she doesn't report it because the security vulnerability could reflect poorly on his or her own performance. This example presents a classic conflict of interest, which can be readily avoided by employing separation of duties.

It is important to understand the responsibilities for policy implementation throughout the seven domains of a typical IT infrastructure and to be able to identify the separation of duties regarding those responsibilities.

In this lab, you will identify the roles and responsibilities for policy implementation, and you will identify the separation of duties for them. You will then create a security management policy that addresses the management and the separation of duties throughout the seven domains of a typical IT infrastructure.

Learning Objectives

Upon completing this lab, you will be able to:

- Identify the roles and responsibilities for policy implementation throughout the seven domains of a typical IT infrastructure.
- Identify the physical separation of duties regarding responsibility for information systems security policy implementation.
- Align responsibilities for policy implementation throughout the seven domains of a typical IT infrastructure.
- Apply separation of duties to a layered security management policy throughout the seven domains of a typical IT infrastructure.
- Create a layered security management policy defining separation of duties.

Deliverables

Upon completion of this lab, you are required to provide the following deliverables to your instructor:

1. Lab Report file;
2. Lab Assessments file.

Hands-On Steps

1. On your local computer, **create** the **lab deliverable files**.

2. **Review** the **Lab Assessment Worksheet**. You will find answers to these questions as you proceed through the lab steps.

3. **Review** the seven domains of a typical IT infrastructure (see Figure 1).

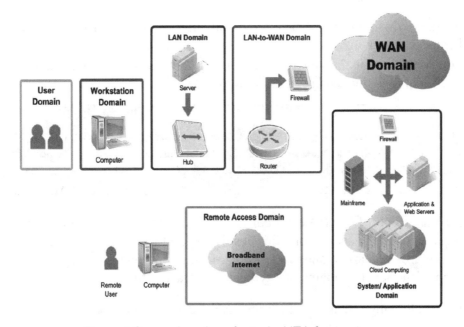

Figure 1 Seven domains of a typical IT infrastructure

4. On your local computer, **open** a new **Internet browser window**.

5. In the address box of your Internet browser, **type** the URL **http://www.sans.org/reading_room/whitepapers/policyissues/building-implementing-information-security-policy_509** and **press Enter** to open the Web site.

6. **Read** the SANS article, "Building and Implementing an Information Security Policy."

7. In your Lab Report file, **explain** the SANS process for building and implementing an information security policy.

8. **Review** the following articles about information security policy implementation. In the address box of your Internet browser, **type** the URL of each article and **press Enter** to open the Web sites:

   • Building and Implementing a Successful Information Security Policy (**http://www.windowsecurity.com/pages/security-policy.pdf**)
   • The Information Security Policies/Computer Security Policies Directory (**http://www.information-security-policies-and-standards.com/**)

9. In your Lab Report file, using the information in these articles and the previous SANS article, **discuss** how you would implement policies in all seven domains of a typical IT infrastructure. **List** the roles and responsibilities of those implementing the policies and those who must follow the policies.

10. **Review** the following information about the separation of duties:

    • No one individual should have too much authority or power to perform a function in a business or organization.
    • Understanding one's domain of responsibilities and where those responsibilities stop is critical to understand separation of duties.

> ▶ **Note:**
> Just because someone has decidedly "too much authority or power" does not mean management will authorize separation of duties to mitigate the risk. The reason is separation of duties essentially means additional labor and/or costs. Instead, management might decide to accept the risk or treat the risk by other means.

11. In your Lab Report file, **create** a security management policy that addresses the management and the separation of duties throughout the seven domains of a typical IT infrastructure. You are to **define** what the information systems security responsibility is for each of the seven domains of a typical IT infrastructure.

12. **Read** the following scenario of the mock XYZ Credit Union/Bank:

    • The organization is a regional XYZ Credit Union/Bank that has multiple branches and locations throughout the region.
    • Online banking and use of the Internet are the bank's strengths, given its limited human resources.
    • The customer service department is the organization's most critical business function.
    • The organization wants to be in compliance with the Gramm-Leach-Bliley Act (GLBA) and IT security best practices regarding its employees.
    • The organization wants to monitor and control use of the Internet by implementing content filtering.
    • The organization wants to eliminate personal use of organization-owned IT assets and systems.

- The organization wants to monitor and control use of the e-mail system by implementing e-mail security controls.
- The organization wants to implement this policy for all the IT assets it owns and to incorporate this policy review into its annual security awareness training.
- The organization wants to define a policy framework, including a security management policy defining the separation of duties for information systems security.

13. Using the following template, in your Lab Report file, **create** a security management policy with defined separation of duties for the XYZ Credit Union/Bank (this should not be longer than three pages):

XYZ Credit Union/Bank

Policy Name

Policy Statement

{Insert policy verbiage here.}

Purpose/Objectives

{Insert the policy's purpose as well as its objectives; include a bulleted list of the policy definitions.}

Scope

{Define whom this policy covers and its scope. Which of the seven domains of a typical IT infrastructure are impacted? All seven must be included in the scope.

What elements, IT assets, or organization-owned assets are within this policy's scope? In this case, you are concerned about which IT assets and elements in each of the domains require information systems security management.}

Standards

{Does the policy statement point to any hardware, software, or configuration standards? If so, list them here and explain the relationship of this policy to these standards. You need to reference technical hardware, software, and configuration standards for IT assets throughout the seven domains of a typical IT infrastructure.}

Procedures

{Explain how you intend to implement this policy for the entire organization. This is important because it is where you must explain and define your separation of duties throughout the seven domains of a typical IT infrastructure. All seven domains must be listed in this section as well as who is responsible for ensuring confidentiality, integrity, and availability (C-I-A) and security policy implementation within that domain.}

Guidelines

{Explain any roadblocks or implementation issues that you must overcome in this section and how you will surmount them per defined guidelines. Any disputes or gaps in the definition and separation of duties responsibility may need to be addressed in this section.}

▶ **Note:**

This completes the lab. **Close** the **Web browser**, if you have not already done so.

Evaluation Criteria and Rubrics

The following are the evaluation criteria for this lab that students must perform:

1. Identify the roles and responsibilities for policy implementation throughout the seven domains of a typical IT infrastructure. – **[20%]**
2. Identify the physical separation of duties regarding responsibility for information systems security policy implementation. – **[20%]**
3. Align responsibilities for policy implementation throughout the seven domains of a typical IT infrastructure. – **[20%]**
4. Apply separation of duties to a layered security management policy throughout the seven domains of a typical IT infrastructure. – **[20%]**
5. Create a layered security management policy defining separation of duties. – **[20%]**

Lab #4 - Assessment Worksheet

Crafting a Layered Security Management Policy—Separation of Duties

Course Name and Number: _____

Student Name: _____

Instructor Name: _____

Lab Due Date: _____

Overview

In this lab, you identified the roles and responsibilities for policy implementation, and you identified the separation of duties for them. You then created a security management policy that addressed the management and the separation of duties throughout the seven domains of a typical IT infrastructure.

Lab Assessment Questions & Answers

1. For each of the seven domains of a typical IT infrastructure, describe a policy you would write and implement for each domain.

2. Describe the roles and responsibilities of those implementing information systems security policies.

3. What does separation of duties mean?

4. How does separation of duties throughout an IT infrastructure mitigate risk for an organization?

5. If a system administrator had both the ID and password to a system, would that be a problem?

6. When using a layered security approach to system administration, who would have the highest access privileges?

7. Who would review the organization's layered approach to security?

8. Why do you only want to refer to technical standards in a policy definition document?

9. Explain why the seven domains of a typical IT infrastructure help organizations align to separation of duties.

10. Why is it important for an organization to have a policy definition for business continuity and disaster recovery?

Lab #5 Crafting an Organization-Wide Security Awareness Training Policy

Introduction

Being only human, most employees will look for the easiest way to do their jobs. If a task seems to be unnecessarily complicated by extra steps—requested by management without an explanation—an employee might very well skip them. An ambitious or creative employee might work harder temporarily but still attempt to find a more efficient or economical way to finish the work.

But what if the extra steps were introduced into the business process for security reasons unknown to the employee? What if those steps, while not the most efficient, helped ensure information was more secure? For these reasons, employees lacking security awareness training tend to introduce risks and vulnerabilities into an organization. This is the untold scenario of why too many companies need to improve their security awareness training. The purpose of an organization-wide security awareness training policy is to mandate annual and periodic security awareness training for new and existing employees.

In this lab, you will identify the risks and threats commonly found in the User and Workstation domains, and you will identify elements of a security awareness training policy as part of an overall layered security strategy. You will create an organization-wide security awareness training policy.

Learning Objectives

Upon completing this lab, you will be able to:

- Identify how risks, threats, and software vulnerabilities impact the seven domains of a typical IT infrastructure.
- Identify the risks and threats commonly found in the User Domain and Workstation Domain.
- Identify the key elements of a security awareness training policy as part of an overall layered security strategy.
- Mitigate the risks and threats identified in the User Domain and Workstation Domain by incorporating these topics into the organization's security awareness training program.
- Create an organization-wide security awareness training policy that mandates annual or periodic security awareness training for new and existing employees.

Deliverables

Upon completion of this lab, you are required to provide the following deliverables to your instructor:

1. Lab Report file;
2. Lab Assessments file.

Hands-On Steps

> ▶ **Note:**
> This is a paper-based lab. To successfully complete the deliverables for this lab, you will need access to Microsoft® Word or another compatible word processor. For some labs, you may also need access to a graphics line drawing application, such as Visio or PowerPoint. Refer to the Preface of this manual for information on creating the lab deliverable files.

1. On your local computer, **create** the **lab deliverable files**.

2. **Review** the **Lab Assessment Worksheet**. You will find answers to these questions as you proceed through the lab steps.

3. On your local computer, **open** a new **Internet browser window**.

4. **Review** the information at the following Web sites. In the address box of your Internet browser, **type** the URL of each and **press Enter** to open the Web sites:

   - Health care: State of North Carolina Department of Health and Human Services (**http://info.dhhs.state.nc.us/olm/manuals/dhs/pol-80/man/06security_training_and_awareness.pdf**)
   - Higher education: University of San Francisco (**http://www.usfca.edu/its/about/policies/awareness/**)
   - Health care: Community Health Plan of Washington (**http://chpw.org/assets/file/Security-Awareness-and-Training-Policy.pdf**)

Great Awareness Policies Make For Lasting Security

The points made here are valuable for any policy, but are arguably most important for a security awareness training policy. How effective your awareness training policy and security training are will directly influence how well your employee values and protects your organization's security position. It is critical that your awareness training policy be well written.

To be sure your policy is effective, answer these questions objectively:

- Is the policy statement as concise and readable as possible, for example, no more than one to three sentences?
- Is the entire policy as concise and readable as possible, for example, no more than two to three pages?
- Does the policy align well with other governing documents?
- Does the policy speak directly to the target audience?
- Does the policy state the "why" with only the minimal detail, and rely on standards or guidelines for the "how"? Write policies in such a way that they won't need frequent updates.
- Does the policy adequately describe scope and responsibilities?
- Are the policy's revision, approval, and distribution documented?

After the policy is approved, the policy's success relies on proper delivery and understanding. To simply give a new employee five minutes to read and sign a policy during orientation is not enough. Focused and interactive "policy understanding" sessions would instead guarantee every employee understands the policy's reasoning and necessity. Customizing these sessions for particular employees by work area can drastically increase how much employees retain and apply the training during their work. Repeat sessions reinforce the policies and keep material fresh in their minds.

5. In your Lab Report file, first **list** the name of the security awareness policy you reviewed, and then **discuss** the policy's main components (do this for each document you researched in the previous step).

6. **Review** the following risks and threats found in the User Domain:

   - Dealing with humans and human nature
   - Dealing with user or employee apathy toward information systems security policy
   - Accessing the Internet and opening "Pandora's box"
   - Surfing the Web, a dangerous trek into unknown territory
   - Opening e-mails and unknown e-mail attachments, which can lead to malicious software and codes
   - Installing unauthorized applications, files, or data onto organization-owned IT assets
   - Downloading applications or software with hidden malicious software or codes
   - Clicking on an unknown URL link that has hidden scripts

7. In your Lab Report file, **identify** a security control or countermeasure to mitigate each risk and threat identified above for the User Domain. Draw from what you read at the URLs in step 4.

8. **Review** the following risks and threats found in the Workstation Domain:

   - Unauthorized access to workstations
   - Operating system software vulnerabilities
   - Application software vulnerabilities
   - Viruses, trojans, worms, spyware, malicious software, and malicious code
   - A user inserting CDs, DVDs, USB thumb drives with personal data and files onto organization-owned IT assets
   - A user downloading unauthorized applications and software onto organization-owned IT assets
   - A user installing unauthorized applications and software onto organization-owned IT assets

9. In your Lab Report file, **identify** a security control or countermeasure to mitigate each risk and threat identified above for the Workstation Domain. Draw from what you read at the URLs in step 4.

▶**Note:**
The above lab steps to identify control measures are exercises in understanding and matching risks to controls.

These controls would not be included as part of a policy, but are rather more appropriate at the guideline level.

10. **Read** the following scenario of the mock XYZ Credit Union/Bank:

- The organization is a regional XYZ Credit Union/Bank that has multiple branches and locations throughout the region.
- Online banking and use of the Internet are the bank's strengths, given its limited human resources.
- The customer service department is the organization's most critical business function.
- The organization wants to be in compliance with the Gramm-Leach-Bliley Act (GLBA) and IT security best practices regarding its employees.
- The organization wants to monitor and control use of the Internet by implementing content filtering.
- The organization wants to eliminate personal use of organization-owned IT assets and systems.
- The organization wants to monitor and control use of the e-mail system by implementing e-mail security controls.
- The organization wants to implement security awareness training policy mandates for all new hires and existing employees. Policy definitions are to include GLBA and customer privacy data requirements, in addition to a mandate for annual security awareness training for all employees.

11. Using the following template, in your Lab Report file, **create** an organization-wide security awareness training policy for the XYZ Credit Union/Bank organization (this should not be longer than three pages):

XYZ Credit Union/Bank

Security Awareness Training Policy

Policy Statement

{Insert policy verbiage here.}

Purpose/Objectives

{Insert the policy's purpose as well as its objectives; use a bulleted list of the policy definition.}

Scope

{Define whom this policy covers and its scope.

Which of the seven domains of a typical IT infrastructure are impacted?

What elements, IT assets, or organization-owned assets are within the scope of this policy?}

Standards

{Does this policy point to any hardware, software, or configuration standards? If so, list them here and explain the relationship of this policy to these standards. In this case, Workstation Domain standards should be referenced; make any necessary assumptions.}

Procedures

{Explain how you intend to implement this policy across the organization and how you intend to deliver annual or ongoing security awareness training for employees.}

Guidelines

{Explain any roadblocks or implementation issues that you must address in this section and how you will overcome them per defined policy guidelines.}

▶ **Note:**
This completes the lab. **Close** the **Web browser**, if you have not already done so.

Evaluation Criteria and Rubrics

The following are the evaluation criteria for this lab that students must perform:

1. Identify how risks, threats, and software vulnerabilities impact the seven domains of a typical IT infrastructure. – **[20%]**
2. Identify the risks and threats commonly found in the User Domain and Workstation Domain. – **[20%]**
3. Identify the key elements of a security awareness training policy as part of an overall layered security strategy. – **[20%]**
4. Mitigate the risks and threats identified in the User Domain and Workstation Domain by incorporating these topics into the organization's security awareness training program. – **[20%]**
5. Create an organization-wide security awareness training policy that mandates annual or periodic security awareness training for new and existing employees. – **[20%]**

Lab #5 - Assessment Worksheet

Crafting an Organization-Wide Security Awareness Training Policy

Course Name and Number: _____

Student Name: _____

Instructor Name: _____

Lab Due Date: _____

Overview

In this lab, you identified the risks and threats commonly found in the User and Workstation domains, and you identified elements of a security awareness training policy as part of an overall layered security strategy. You created an organization-wide security awareness training policy.

Lab Assessment Questions & Answers

1. How does a security awareness training policy impact an organization's capability to mitigate risks, threats, and vulnerabilities?

2. Why do you need a security awareness training policy if you have new hires attend or participate in the organization's security awareness training program during new hire orientation?

3. What is the relationship between an acceptable use policy (AUP) and a security awareness training policy?

4. Why is it important to prevent users from engaging in downloading or installing applications and software found on the Internet?

5. When trying to combat software vulnerabilities in the Workstation Domain, what is needed most to deal with operating system, application, and other software installations?

6. Why is it important to educate users about the risks, threats, and vulnerabilities found on the Internet and World Wide Web?

7. What are some strategies for preventing users or employees from downloading and installing rogue applications and software found on the Internet?

8. What is one strategy for preventing users from clicking on unknown e-mail attachments and files?

9. Why should you include organization-wide policies in employee security awareness training?

10. Why does an organization need a policy on conducting security awareness training annually and periodically?

11. What other strategies can organizations implement to keep security awareness top of mind with all employees and authorized users?

12. Why should an organization provide updated security awareness training when a new policy is implemented throughout the User Domain or Workstation Domain?

Lab #6 Defining a Remote Access Policy to Support Remote Health Care Clinics

Introduction

Employing the Internet's cheap connectivity presents both opportunities and challenges for businesses. The challenges include an organization's security and compliance while allowing remote access to the employees.

In many businesses, administrators, staff, and, in some cases, customers are granted remote access into the organization's protected, private Local Area Network (LAN). This introduces not only the same risks inherent with authenticated users on the local network but additional risks by granting local access to users from the Internet's open network.

In this lab, you will identify the risks and threats commonly found in the Remote Access Domain, and you will define the scope of a remote access policy as it relates to the Remote Access Domain. You will mitigate the risks and threats found in the Remote Access Domain, and you will create a remote access policy that incorporates a policy statement, standards, procedures, and guidelines.

Learning Objectives

Upon completing this lab, you will be able to:

- Define the scope of a remote access policy as it relates to the Remote Access Domain.
- Identify the key elements of a remote access policy within an organization as part of an overall security management framework.
- Align the remote access policy with the organization's goals for compliance.
- Identify proper security controls and countermeasures for risks and threats found within the Remote Access Domain as defined in the remote access policy definition.
- Create a remote access policy definition incorporating a policy statement, standards, procedures, and guidelines.

45

Deliverables

Upon completion of this lab, you are required to provide the following deliverables to your instructor:

1. Lab Report file;
2. Lab Assessments file.

Hands-On Steps

> ▶**Note:**
> This is a paper-based lab. To successfully complete the deliverables for this lab, you will need access to Microsoft® Word or another compatible word processor. For some labs, you may also need access to a graphics line drawing application, such as Visio or PowerPoint. Refer to the Preface of this manual for information on creating the lab deliverable files.

1. On your local computer, **create** the **lab deliverable files**.

2. **Review** the **Lab Assessment Worksheet**. You will find answers to these questions as you proceed through the lab steps.

3. On your local computer, **open** a new **Internet browser window**.

4. In the address box of your Internet browser, **type** the following URLs and **press Enter** to open the Web sites to **review** the sample remote access policy documents:

   - SANS Institute: Remote Access Policy template (**http://www.sans.org/security-resources/policies/Remote_Access_Policy.pdf**)
   - Higher education: Clark University (**http://www.clarku.edu/offices/its/policies/remoteaccess.cfm**)
   - Higher education: Purdue University (**http://www.purdue.edu/policies/index.html**). **Type remote access policy** in the **Search Policies box** in the top right corner of the Web page. **Browse** the available links on the resulting search page, and **click** on a link relating to the university's remote access policy.
   - Health care provider: Ashford and St. Peter's Hospitals (**http://www.asph.nhs.uk/attachments/article/3246/Remote%20access%20policy.pdf**)

> ▶**Note:**
> The differing outlines for both higher education remote access policies are a reminder that a policy can be proper and effective without having to follow a strict structure.
>
> How the hospital's remote access policy is structured is the clearest reminder that the Remote Access Domain is technically the same as the User Domain, only with the added burden of transmitting over an insecure network. User authentication becomes remote authentication.

5. **Review** the following risks and threats found in the Remote Access Domain:

   - Brute force user ID and password attacks
   - Users or employees unaware of the risks, threats, and dangers of the Internet and shared Wi-Fi or broadband Internet access

- Multiple access attempts and logon retries
- Unauthorized access to IT systems, applications, and data
- Privacy data or confidential data is compromised remotely
- Data leakage occurs in violation of data classification standard
- A remote worker's laptop is stolen
- A remote worker's token device is stolen
- A remote worker requires access to the patient medical records system through the public Internet

6. In your Lab Report file, **identify** a security control or countermeasure to mitigate each risk and threat identified in the Remote Access Domain. These security controls or security countermeasures will become the basis of the scope of the Remote Access Domain policy definition to help mitigate the risks and threats commonly found within the Remote Access Domain.

> ▶ **Note:**
> In real-world environments, ensure that controls, countermeasures, and incident responses are aligned between similar scenarios in the Remote Access Domain and the User Domain. This is important because remote connectivity and users can pose many of the same threats.

7. **Review** the following characteristics of the mock XYZ Health Care Provider:

- Regional XYZ Health Care Provider has multiple, remote health care branches and locations throughout the region.
- Online access to patients' medical records through the public Internet is required for remote nurses and hospices providing in-home medical services.
- Online access to patients' medical records from remote clinics is done through Secure Sockets Layer Virtual Private Network (SSL VPN) secure Web application front-end through the public Internet.
- The organization wants to be in compliance with the Health Insurance Portability and Accountability Act (HIPAA) and IT security best practices regarding remote access through the public Internet in the Remote Access Domain.
- The organization wants to monitor and control the use of remote access by implementing system logging and VPN connections.
- The organization wants to implement a security awareness training policy mandating that all new hires and existing employees obtain remote access security training. Policy definition to include HIPAA and electronic protected health information (ePHI) security requirements and a mandate for annual security awareness training for all remote or mobile employees.

8. Using the following template, in your Lab Report file, **create** an organization-wide remote access policy for XYZ Health Care Provider (this should not be longer than three pages):

XYZ Health Care Provider

Remote Access Policy for Remote Workers & Medical Clinics

Policy Statement

{Insert policy verbiage here.}

Purpose/Objectives

{Insert the policy's purpose as well as its objectives; use a bulleted list of the policy definition.}

Scope

{Define this policy's scope and whom it covers.

Which of the seven domains of a typical IT infrastructure are impacted?

What elements, IT assets, or organization-owned assets are within the scope of this policy?}

Standards

{Does this policy point to any hardware, software, or configuration standards? If so, list them here, and explain the relationship of this policy to these standards. In this case, Remote Access Domain standards should be referenced, such as encryption standards, SSL VPN standards—make any necessary assumptions.}

Procedures

{Explain how you intend to implement this policy organization-wide and how you intend to deliver the annual or ongoing security awareness training for remote workers and mobile employees.}

Guidelines

{Explain any roadblocks or implementation issues that you must address in this section and how you will overcome them per defined policy guidelines.}

▶**Note:**
This completes the lab. **Close** the **Web browser**, if you have not already done so.

Evaluation Criteria and Rubrics

The following are the evaluation criteria for this lab that students must perform:

1. Define the scope of a remote access policy as it relates to the Remote Access Domain. – **[20%]**
2. Identify the key elements of a remote access policy within an organization as part of an overall security management framework. – **[20%]**
3. Align the remote access policy with the organization's goals for compliance. – **[20%]**
4. Identify proper security controls and countermeasures for risks and threats found within the Remote Access Domain as defined in the remote access policy definition. – **[20%]**
5. Create a remote access policy definition incorporating a policy statement, standards, procedures, and guidelines. – **[20%]**

Lab #6 - Assessment Worksheet

Defining a Remote Access Policy to Support Remote Health Care Clinics

Course Name and Number: _____

Student Name: _____

Instructor Name: _____

Lab Due Date: _____

Overview

In this lab, you identified the risks and threats commonly found in the Remote Access Domain, and you defined the scope of a remote access policy as it relates to the Remote Access Domain. You mitigated the risks and threats found in the Remote Access Domain, and you created a remote access policy that incorporated a policy statement, standards, procedures, and guidelines.

Lab Assessment Questions & Answers

1. What are the biggest risks when using the public Internet as a Wide Area Network (WAN) or transport for remote access to your organization's IT infrastructure?

2. Why does the mock XYZ Health Care Provider need to define a remote access policy to properly implement remote access through the public Internet?

3. One of the major prerequisites for the mock health care organization scenario is the requirement to support nurses and health care professionals who are mobile and who visit patients in their homes. Another requirement is for remote clinics to access a shared patient medical records system via a Web browser. Which type of secure remote VPN solution is recommended for these two types of remote access?

4. Why is it important to mobile workers and users to know what the risks, threats, and vulnerabilities are when conducting remote access through the public Internet?

5. Which domain (not the Remote Access Domain) throughout the seven domains of a typical IT infrastructure supports remote access connectivity for users and mobile workers needing to connect to the organization's IT infrastructure?

6. Where are the implementation instructions defined in a remote access policy definition? Does this section describe how to support the two different remote access users and requirements as described in this lab's XYZ Health Care Provider scenario?

7. A remote clinic has a requirement to upload ePHI data from the clinic to the organization's IT infrastructure on a daily basis in a batch-processing format. How should this remote access requirement be handled within or outside of this remote access policy definition?

8. Why is a remote access policy definition a best practice for handling remote employees and authorized users who require remote access from home or on business trips?

9. Why is it a best practice of a remote access policy definition to require employees and users to fill in a separate VPN remote access authorization form?

10. Why is it important to align standards, procedures, and guidelines for a remote access policy definition?

11. What security controls, monitoring, and logging should be enabled for remote VPN access and users?

12. Should an organization mention that it will be monitoring and logging remote access use in its remote access policy definition?

Lab #7 Identifying Necessary Policies for Business Continuity—BIA and Recovery Time Objectives

Introduction

The purpose of a business impact analysis (BIA) is to assess and align affected IT systems, applications, and resources to their required recovery time objectives (RTOs). The prioritization of the identified mission-critical business functions defines what IT systems, applications, and resources are impacted. The RTO drives the type of business continuity and recovery steps needed to maintain IT operations in specified time frames. The business continuity plan (BCP) outlines these steps so that operations may continue when mission-critical functions are at risk or jeopardized.

In this lab, you will identify a BCP's elements, you will review the results of a BIA and RTOs, and you will create a BCP.

Learning Objectives

Upon completing this lab, you will be able to:

- Identify the major elements of a business continuity plan (BCP).
- Align a business continuity plan's major elements with required policy definitions.
- Review the results of a qualitative business impact analysis (BIA) for a mock organization.
- Review the results of defined recovery time objectives (RTOs) for mission-critical business functions and applications.
- Create a BCP policy defining an organization's prioritized business functions from the BIA with assigned RTOs.

53

Deliverables

Upon completion of this lab, you are required to provide the following deliverables to your instructor:

1. Lab Report file;
2. Lab Assessments file.

Hands-On Steps

►**Note:**
This is a paper-based lab. To successfully complete the deliverables for this lab, you will need access to Microsoft® Word or another compatible word processor. For some labs, you may also need access to a graphics line drawing application, such as Visio or PowerPoint. Refer to the Preface of this manual for information on creating the lab deliverable files.

1. On your local computer, **create** the **lab deliverable files**.

2. **Review** the **Lab Assessment Worksheet**. You will find answers to these questions as you proceed through the lab steps.

3. On your local computer, **open** a new **Internet browser window**.

4. In the address box of your Internet browser, **type** the URL **http://www.ready.gov/business/implementation/continuity** and **press Enter** to open the Web site.

5. **Read** the "Business Continuity Plan" article.

6. In your Lab Report file, **describe** what a BCP is and **list** the steps for developing a BCP.

7. In the address box of your Internet browser, **type** the URL **http://www.ready.gov/business-impact-analysis** and **press Enter** to open the Web site.

8. **Read** the "Business Impact Analysis" article.

9. In your Lab Report file, **describe** what a BIA is, how you conduct one, and how the BIA is related to the BCP.

►**Note:**
Conducting a BIA entails describing any mission-critical business functions and processes. The next step is to identify all threats and vulnerabilities. Once you have both of these deliverables, you can compare the findings with the organization's existing policies. What stands out are the areas in your policies needing improvement.

BIAs are a reoccurring analysis, sometimes done once a year. BIAs are revisited because as a business and/or the market changes, the assets and processes deemed critical change. Moreover, recovery times might grow or tighten.

10. **Review** the following sample BIA template:

Business Function or Process	Business Impact Factor	IT Systems/Apps Infrastructure Impacts	RTO/RPO
Internal and external voice communications with customers in real-time			
Internal and external e-mail communications with customers via store and forward messaging			
Domain Name Server (DNS) for internal and external Internet Protocol (IP) communications			
Internet connectivity for e-mail and store and forward customer service			
Self-service Web site for customer access to information and personal account information			
e-Commerce site for online customer purchases or scheduling 24x7x365			
Payroll and human resources for employees			
Real-time customer service via Web site, e-mail, or telephone requires customer relationship management (CRM)			
Network management and technical support			

Marketing and events			
Sales orders or customer/student registration			
Remote branch office sales order entry to headquarters			
Voice and e-mail communications to remote branches			
Accounting and finance support: Accounts payable, Accounts receivable, etc.			

11. In your Lab Report file, **fill in the BIA template** as follows:

- In the Business Impact Factor column: **Assign** a business impact factor of **Critical**, **Major**, **Minor**, or **None** to each business function or process.
- In the IT Systems/Apps Infrastructure Impacts column: **Identify** the IT systems and applications impacted by the business function (for example, determine what would be affected if the function or process failed).

12. **Review** the following metrics of the BCP policy definition:

- **Recovery Time Objective (RTO):** Defines how quickly IT systems, servers, applications, and access to data services and processes must be operational following some kind of incident, including recovery of applications and data and end-user access to those applications
- **Recovery Point Objective (RPO):** Defines the point in time that marks the end of the period during which data can still be recovered using backups, journals, or transaction logs

> **▶ Note:**
> To best understand the difference between RTO versus RPO, ask yourself these two questions:
>
> - If your data center blew up, how much time can pass before your business is doomed? That's your RTO.
> - If your backups are failing, how far back can your backup losses go before business is ruined? That's your RPO.

13. **Review** the following RTO and RPO metrics for the BIA:

Critical	RTO: 8 hours	RPO: 0 hours
Major	RTO: 24 hours	RPO: 8 hours
Minor	RTO: 1 week	RPO: 3 days
None	RTO: 1 month	RPO: 7 days

14. In your Lab Report file, **fill in the BIA template** as follows based on what you read in the previous steps:

   - In the RTO/RPO column: **Assign** an RTO/RPO to each of the business functions or processes.

▶ **Note:**
An important difference between RTO and RPO is the purpose behind each. Your RTO determines your business continuity management plan and how much money you need to resume operations. The RPO only affects your backup operations.

15. Using the following template, in your Lab Report file, **create** a business continuity plan policy definition/business impact analysis for the mock XYZ Credit Union/Bank (this should not be longer than three pages). In the plan, reference the RTO and RPO standards in the policy's Standards section:

XYZ Credit Union/Bank

Policy Name

Policy Statement

{Insert policy verbiage here.}

Purpose/Objectives

{Insert the policy's purpose as well as its objectives; use a bulleted list of the policy definition. This should mirror the purpose/objectives of a business impact analysis (BIA).}

Scope

{Define this policy's scope and whom it covers.

Within a BCP outline, what are this policy's scope and boundaries?

What elements or criteria are within this policy's scope?}

How to Gain Approval for Your Plan

The first step toward implementing your business continuity plan (BCP) lies in gaining executive management's wholehearted support. You can't wait to win this approval until after you've drawn up and presented your plan to management. You must make clear to management from the get-go the costs associated with any lasting disruptions to business and the pressing need for every business to have a BCP to protect itself.

To win executive management's endorsement of your BCP, research the costs associated with business disruptions, the costs of implementing a business continuity plan, and the steps for continuity and recovery that are specific to your organization, and then use this data to strengthen the arguments for implementing your plan. Also, ask management what it is looking for. Understand the executives' short- and long-term concerns and what concrete benefits they are looking for from a BCP. Find out as well how much they are willing and able to invest in such a plan. Remind them that while a BCP requires ongoing upgrades, which will also come with a price tag, to go without such a plan and its upgrades could result in even longer and far costlier business disruptions.

To win executive management support takes proper planning. Too many well-intentioned managers and consultants devote all their time on their plan's presentation and not enough time consulting with management. Use information from your conversations with management to plan your approach, presentation materials, and time. Remember, you'll likely get just one try at this.

Standards

{Does this policy point to any hardware, software, or configuration standards? In this case, you need to reference the recovery time objectives (RTOs) and recovery point objectives (RPOs) as standards and metrics within the policy definition itself. List them here and explain the relationship of this policy to these standards.}

Procedures

{Explain how you intend to implement this policy across the entire organization.}

Guidelines

{Explain any roadblocks or implementation issues that you must address in this section and how you will overcome them per defined policy guidelines.}

▶ **Note:**
This completes the lab. **Close** the **Web browser**, if you have not already done so.

Evaluation Criteria and Rubrics

The following are the evaluation criteria for this lab that students must perform:

1. Identify the major elements of a business continuity plan (BCP). – **[20%]**
2. Align a business continuity plan's major elements with required policy definitions. – **[20%]**
3. Review the results of a qualitative business impact analysis (BIA) for a mock organization. – **[20%]**
4. Review the results of defined recovery time objectives (RTOs) for mission-critical business functions and applications. – **[20%]**
5. Create a BCP policy defining an organization's prioritized business functions from the BIA with assigned RTOs. – **[20%]**

Lab #7 - Assessment Worksheet

Identifying Necessary Policies for Business Continuity—BIA and Recovery Time Objectives

Course Name and Number: _____

Student Name: _____

Instructor Name: _____

Lab Due Date: _____

Overview

In this lab, you identified a BCP's elements, you reviewed the results of a BIA and RTOs, and you created a BCP.

Lab Assessment Questions & Answers

1. Why must an organization define policies for its business continuity and disaster recovery plans?

2. When should you define a policy and when should you not define one?

3. What is the purpose of having a BCP policy definition that defines the organization's BIA?

4. Why is it critical to align the RTO and RPO standards within the policy definition itself?

5. What is the purpose of a BIA?

6. Why is a BIA an important first step in defining a BCP?

7. How do risk management and risk assessment relate to a business impact analysis for an IT infrastructure?

8. True or false: If the recovery point objective (RPO) metric is not the same as the recovery time objective (RTO), you may potentially lose data or not have data backed up to recover. This represents a gap in potential lost or unrecoverable data.

9. Why should organizations update their BCP, BIA, RTOs, and RPOs?

10. For the sample BIA, which systems, applications, and functions were mission-critical to this organization?

Lab #8 Crafting a Security or Computer Incident Response Policy—CIRT Response Team

Introduction

Regardless of whether an organization's policies are perfect, the staff is superior, or the walls are impenetrable, a time will come when an incident occurs. Whether it's a security breach or an employee is exploited by social engineering, an incident will take place and the organization had better be prepared for it.

In this lab, you will define the purpose of a security or computer incident response team (CIRT), you will identify major elements of a security or computer incident response methodology, you will align the roles and responsibilities to elements of a CIRT response team, you will identify critical management, human resources, legal, IT, and information systems security personnel required for the CIRT response team, and you will create a CIRT response policy definition that defines the CIRT response team's purpose and goal and the authority granted during an incident.

Learning Objectives

Upon completing this lab, you will be able to:

- Define the purpose of a security or computer incident response team.
- Identify the major elements of a security or computer incident response methodology.
- Align the roles and responsibilities to elements of a CIRT response team.
- Identify critical management, human resources, legal, IT, and information systems security personnel required for the CIRT response team.
- Create a CIRT response policy definition that defines the CIRT response team's purpose and goal and the authority granted during an incident.

Deliverables

Upon completion of this lab, you are required to provide the following deliverables to your instructor:

1. Lab Report file;
2. Lab Assessments file.

Hands-On Steps

> ▶**Note:**
> This is a paper-based lab. To successfully complete the deliverables for this lab, you will need access to Microsoft® Word or another compatible word processor. For some labs, you may also need access to a graphics line drawing application, such as Visio or PowerPoint. Refer to the Preface of this manual for information on creating the lab deliverable files.

1. On your local computer, **create** the **lab deliverable files**.

2. **Review** the **Lab Assessment Worksheet**. You will find answers to these questions as you proceed through the lab steps.

3. On your local computer, **open** a new **Internet browser window**.

4. Using your favorite search engine, **search** for a **sample incident response plan**.

5. **Review** the plan.

6. In your Lab Report file, **describe** the policy definitions that are required with a security or computer incident response plan. Use the sample plan to **explain** the purpose of policy definitions.

7. In the address box of your Internet browser, **type** the URL **http://www.oas.org/cyber/documents/IRM-5-Malicious-Network-Behaviour.pdf and press Enter to open the Web site.**

8. **Review** the six steps listed on the Web site.

9. In the address box of your Internet browser, **type** the URL **http://my.safaribooksonline.com/book/networking/incident-response/1578702569/a-methodology-for-incident-response/ch03lev1sec2 and press Enter to open the Web site.**

10. **Review** the six steps listed on the Web site.

11. In the address box of your Internet browser, **type** the URL **http://www.uwinnipeg.ca/index/info-security-incident-response-procedures and press Enter to open the Web site.**

12. **Read** the following three sections on the University of Winnipeg page: Methodology, Roles of Involved Parties, and Classifying Incident Levels.

13. In your Lab Report file, **describe** the purpose of a security or computer incident response plan.

14. In your Lab Report file, **outline** the six-step methodology for performing incident response. **List** each step and its purpose.

15. In your Lab Report file, **describe** how UWinnipeg mitigates risks and threats by having a security or incident response plan and team.

16. **Review** the following definition of chain of custody and integrity of physical evidence in a court of law:

   • Chain of custody: The movement and location of physical evidence from the time it is obtained until the time it is presented in court

---

▶**Note:**

It is impossible to know at the beginning of any incident if the case might become a court case. Treat every incident response assuming evidence documentation is required.

---

17. In your Lab Report file, **describe** the need for a security or computer incident response team policy definition that addresses the delegation of authority to the CIRT response team members during an incident response emergency.

▶**Note:**

Remember, in terms of responding to and handling an incident, who is the provider of information and who is the consumer. Senior management approves the response policy and budget, but it does not possess the subject matter expertise to handle the incident. Meanwhile, the incident response team should only make recommendations to management, not make decisions that might impact business. It is up to senior management to either give or deny approval.

Management remains the consumer and chief decider, based on information provided to it by the experts.

---

18. **Review** the following characteristics of the mock XYZ Credit Union/Bank:

   • The organization is a regional XYZ Credit Union/Bank that has multiple branches and locations throughout the region.
   • Online banking and use of the Internet are the bank's strengths, given its limited human resources.
   • The customer service department is the organization's most critical business function.
   • The organization wants to be in compliance with the Gramm-Leach-Bliley Act (GLBA) and IT security best practices regarding its employees.
   • The organization wants to monitor and control use of the Internet by implementing content filtering.
   • The organization wants to eliminate personal use of organization-owned IT assets and systems.
   • The organization wants to monitor and control use of the e-mail system by implementing e-mail security controls.

- The organization wants to implement this policy for all the IT assets it owns and to incorporate this policy review into its annual security awareness training.
- The organization wants to create a security or computer incident response team to deal with security breaches and other incidents if attacked providing full authority for the team to perform whatever activities are needed to maintain chain of custody in performing forensics and evidence collection.
- The organization wants to implement this policy throughout the organization to provide full authority during crisis to the CIRT team members over all physical facilities, IT assets, IT systems, applications, and data owned by the organization.

19. Using the following template, in your Lab Report file, **create** a computer incident response policy granting team members full access and authority to perform forensics and to maintain a chain of custody for physical evidence containment. Create this policy for the XYZ Credit Union/Bank (this should not be longer than three pages):

XYZ Credit Union/Bank

Computer Incident Response Team—Access & Authorization Policy

Policy Statement

{Insert policy verbiage here.}

Purpose/Objectives

{Insert the policy's purpose as well as its objectives; use a bulleted list of the policy definition. Define the security incident response team members and the authorization and authority granted to them during a crisis or securing incident situation.}

Scope

{Define this policy's scope and whom it covers.

Which of the seven domains of a typical IT infrastructure are impacted?

What elements, IT assets, or organization-owned assets are within the scope of this policy?

What access and authority are granted to the incident response team members that may be outside of standard protocol?}

Standards

{Does this policy point to any hardware, software, or configuration standards? If so, list them here and explain the relationship of this policy to these standards.}

Procedures

{Explain how you intend to implement this policy across the organization.

Also, define and incorporate the six-step incident response approach here along with how the chain of custody must be maintained throughout any evidence collection process.}

Guidelines

{Explain any roadblocks or implementation issues that you must address in this section and how you will overcome them per defined policy guidelines.}

▶ **Note:**
This completes the lab. **Close** the **Web browser**, if you have not already done so.

Evaluation Criteria and Rubrics

The following are the evaluation criteria for this lab that students must perform:

1. Define the purpose of a security or computer incident response team. – **[20%]**
2. Identify the major elements of a security or computer incident response methodology. – **[20%]**
3. Align the roles and responsibilities to elements of a CIRT response team. – **[20%]**
4. Identify critical management, human resources, legal, IT, and information systems security personnel required for the CIRT response team. – **[20%]**
5. Create a CIRT response policy definition that defines the CIRT response team's purpose and goal and the authority granted during an incident. – **[20%]**

Lab #8 - Assessment Worksheet

Crafting a Security or Computer Incident Response Policy—CIRT Response Team

Course Name and Number: _____

Student Name: _____

Instructor Name: _____

Lab Due Date: _____

Overview

In this lab, you defined the purpose of a security or computer incident response team (CIRT), you identified major elements of a security or computer incident response methodology, you aligned the roles and responsibilities to elements of a CIRT response team, you identified critical management, human resources, legal, IT, and information systems security personnel required for the CIRT response team, and you created a CIRT response policy definition that defines the CIRT response team's purpose and goal and the authority granted during an incident.

Lab Assessment Questions & Answers

1. What are the six steps in the incident response methodology?

2. If an organization has no intention of prosecuting a perpetrator or attacker, does it still need an incident response team to handle forensics?

3. Why is it a good idea to include human resources on the incident response management team?

4. Why is it a good idea to include legal or general counsel on the incident response management team?

5. How do an incident response plan and incident response team help reduce risks to the organization?

6. If you are reacting to a malicious software attack, such as a virus and its spread, during which step in the incident response process are you attempting to minimize its spreading?

7. When a security incident has been declared, does a PC technician have full access and authority to seize and confiscate a vice president's laptop computer? Why or why not?

8. For which step in the incident response methodology should you document the steps and procedures to replicate the solution?

9. Why is a post-mortem review of an incident the most important step in the incident response methodology?

10. Why is a policy definition required for a computer security incident response team?

Lab #9 Assessing and Auditing an Existing IT Security Policy Framework Definition

Introduction

Your policies should be born from a well-thought-out framework. In fact, the process of writing policies for your business begins with crafting a framework. The framework should outline how each policy will address different risks to the business. It can be a good idea to overlap your policies, since that provides defense in depth. In addition, a framework isn't ironclad; it should be updated when you discover new or evolving risks. For example, if a gap analysis finds deficiencies in an organization's policies, it is necessary to amend both framework and policies.

This lab will demonstrate how to assess and audit an IT security policy framework definition by performing a gap analysis with remediation. Most policy definitions cover identified risks, threats, and vulnerabilities. Some have gaps, however, that must be mitigated with recommendations for other IT security policies.

In this lab, you will identify risks, threats, and vulnerabilities in the seven domains of a typical IT infrastructure, you will review existing IT security policies as part of a policy framework definition, you will align IT security policies throughout the seven domains of a typical IT infrastructure as part of a layered security strategy, you will identify gaps in the IT security policy framework definition, and you will recommend other IT security policies that can help mitigate all known risks, threats, and vulnerabilities throughout the seven domains of a typical IT infrastructure.

Learning Objectives

Upon completing this lab, you will be able to:

- Identify risks, threats, and vulnerabilities in the seven domains of a typical IT infrastructure.
- Review existing IT security policies as part of a policy framework definition.
- Align IT security policies throughout the seven domains of a typical IT infrastructure as part of a layered security strategy.
- Identify gaps in the IT security policy framework definition.
- Recommend other IT security policies that can help mitigate all known risks, threats, and vulnerabilities throughout the seven domains of a typical IT infrastructure.

Deliverables

Upon completion of this lab, you are required to provide the following deliverables to your instructor:

1. Lab Report file;
2. Lab Assessments file.

Hands-On Steps

> ▶ **Note:**
> This is a paper-based lab. To successfully complete the deliverables for this lab, you will need access to Microsoft® Word or another compatible word processor. For some labs, you may also need access to a graphics line drawing application, such as Visio or PowerPoint. Refer to the Preface of this manual for information on creating the lab deliverable files.

1. On your local computer, **create** the **lab deliverable files**.

2. **Review** the **Lab Assessment Worksheet**. You will find answers to these questions as you proceed through the lab steps.

3. **Review** the following risks, threats, and vulnerabilities commonly found throughout the seven domains of a typical IT infrastructure. You will fill in the column at right later in this lab:

Risks, Threats, and Vulnerabilities	Policy or Recommended IT Security Policy
Unauthorized access from public Internet	
User destroys data in application and deletes all files	
Hacker penetrates IT infrastructure and gains access to internal network	
Intraoffice employee romance gone bad	
Fire destroys primary data center	
Communication circuit outages	
Workstation operating system (OS) has a known software vulnerability	
Unauthorized access to organization-owned workstations	
Loss of production data	
Denial of service attack on the organization's e-mail server	
Remote communications from home office	
Local Area Network (LAN) server OS has a known software vulnerability	
User downloads an unknown e-mail attachment	
Workstation browser has software vulnerability	
Service provider has a major network outage	
Weak ingress/egress traffic filtering degrades performance	
User inserts CDs and USB hard drives with personal photos, music, and videos on organization-owned computers	
Virtual Private Network (VPN) tunneling between remote computer and ingress/egress router	
Wireless Local Area Network (WLAN) access points are needed for LAN connectivity within a warehouse	
Need to prevent rogue users from unauthorized WLAN access	

Value of Risk-Based Policy Development

In the previous table, you will only be providing a policy relevant to the risk, threat, or vulnerability. No risk assessment or suggested control is required. However, those would normally be the necessary next steps.

Familiarity with the risks, threats, and vulnerabilities faced by your organization is the foundation for developing appropriate policies to address those risks. This is called a risk-based approach. The process begins with focusing on the worst threats to the business.

In terms of compliance, regulators want your business to be able to quickly identify and assess risks. When your policy development is risk-based, your business satisfies regulators more easily than a business writing policies from another method such as cost-based. For example, the Health Insurance Portability and Accountability Act (HIPAA) requires a risk-based approach.

4. An IT security policy framework outlines the policies, their standards and guidelines, and the procedures necessary for directing an organization's security responses to risks, threats, and vulnerabilities commonly found in an IT infrastructure. **Review** the Defining an Information Systems Security Policy Framework for an IT Infrastructure lab and the Crafting a Layered Security Management Policy—Separation of Duties lab in this lab manual for the policy definitions you wrote and the basic requirements of policies, the benefits of them, the control factors, and policies every organization needs.

5. On your local computer, **open** a new **Internet browser window**.

6. Using your favorite search engine, **research** each of the policies listed in the IT security policy framework definition chart below (Figure 1).

Figure 1 IT security policy framework definition

7. In your Lab Report file, **write** a definition for each policy. **Include** in your definition a standard or guideline that the policy might contain and a procedure that might result because of the policy.

   In your Lab Report file, **fill in** the Policy or Recommended IT Security Policy column in the chart from step 3. **Select** an appropriate policy from the IT security policy framework definition chart to **align** each risk, threat, and vulnerability with a policy that should explain how to respond to it. If there isn't an appropriate policy, then **identify** that as a gap. For any risk you don't match to a policy, insert a recommendation for an IT security policy that can eliminate the gap.

> ▶**Note:**
> By learning to associate risks with a particular policy, you will also develop a keen eye for identifying gaps or weak points in your policies. This is how you will become a better policy writer.

8. In the address box of your Internet browser, **type** the following URLs that include articles about layered security and then **press Enter** to open each Web site:

   - TechRepublic: **http://www.techrepublic.com/blog/security/understanding-layered-security-and-defense-in-depth/703**
   - SANS Institute: **http://www.giac.org/paper/gsec/2599/layered-security/104465**
   - SANS Institute: **http://www.giac.org/paper/gsec/722/layered-authentication/101620**
   - Symantec: **http://www.symantec.com/connect/blogs/layered-security-strategy-key-trust**

9. In your Lab Report file, **write** a summary paper that outlines what is involved in a layered security plan, how it benefits organizations, and explain how policies fit into a layered security strategy.

> ▶**Note:**
> This completes the lab. **Close** the **Web browser**, if you have not already done so.

Evaluation Criteria and Rubrics

The following are the evaluation criteria for this lab that students must perform:

1. Identify risks, threats, and vulnerabilities in the seven domains of a typical IT infrastructure. – **[20%]**
2. Review existing IT security policies as part of a policy framework definition. – **[20%]**
3. Align IT security policies throughout the seven domains of a typical IT infrastructure as part of a layered security strategy. – **[20%]**
4. Identify gaps in the IT security policy framework definition. – **[20%]**
5. Recommend other IT security policies that can help mitigate all known risks, threats, and vulnerabilities throughout the seven domains of a typical IT infrastructure. – **[20%]**

Lab #9 - Assessment Worksheet

Assessing and Auditing an Existing IT Security Policy Framework Definition

Course Name and Number: _____

Student Name: _____

Instructor Name: _____

Lab Due Date: _____

Overview

In this lab, you identified risks, threats, and vulnerabilities in the seven domains of a typical IT infrastructure, you reviewed existing IT security policies as part of a policy framework definition, you aligned IT security policies throughout the seven domains of a typical IT infrastructure as part of a layered security strategy, you identified gaps in the IT security policy framework definition, and you recommended other IT security policies that could help mitigate all known risks, threats, and vulnerabilities throughout the seven domains of a typical IT infrastructure.

Lab Assessment Questions & Answers

1. What is the purpose of having a policy framework definition?

2. When should you use a policy definition as a means of risk mitigation and as an element of a layered security strategy?

3. In your gap analysis of the IT security policy framework definition, which risks did not align with a policy?

4. Do you think you need policies for your Internet service providers? Explain your answer.

5. Which polices from the list provided in this lab would help optimize performance of an organization's Internet connection?

6. Why should you use a layered security approach? Cite the articles you read when answering this question.

7. How does an IT security policy framework make it easier to monitor and enforce policies throughout an organization?

Lab #10 Aligning an IT Security Policy Framework to the Seven Domains of a Typical IT Infrastructure

Introduction

Consider an established organization, which created a complete policy framework years ago. The company has, under your guidance, developed a risk-based policy development program to ensure that the policy framework is current. In fact, the team assigned to the task recently identified and addressed policy gaps discovered during the last risk assessment. The overarching framework now demonstrates complete coverage, including defense in depth between policies. However, you've left that company and are about to start work at a new bank. The bank would like your expertise to create the same IT security policy framework, aligned with its infrastructure and compliance needs.

In this lab, you will define the policy statement for various IT security policy definitions, you will identify the key elements of IT security policy definitions as part of a framework definition, you will reference key standards and requirements for IT security policy definitions, you will incorporate procedures and guidelines into an IT security policy definition example needed to fill a gap in a framework definition, and you will create an IT security policy definition for a risk mitigation solution for an IT security policy framework definition.

Learning Objectives

Upon completing this lab, you will be able to:

- Define the policy statement for various IT security policy definitions.
- Identify key elements of IT security policy definitions as part of a framework definition.
- Reference key standards and requirements for IT security policy definitions needed for a framework definition.
- Incorporate procedures and guidelines into an IT security policy definition example needed to fill a gap in a framework definition.
- Create an IT security policy definition for a risk mitigation solution for an IT security policy framework definition.

Deliverables

Upon completion of this lab, you are required to provide the following deliverables to your instructor:

1. Lab Report file;
2. Lab Assessments file.

Hands-On Steps

> ▶ **Note:**
> This is a paper-based lab. To successfully complete the deliverables for this lab, you will need access to Microsoft® Word or another compatible word processor. For some labs, you may also need access to a graphics line drawing application, such as Visio or PowerPoint. Refer to the Preface of this manual for information on creating the lab deliverable files.

1. On your local computer, **create** the **lab deliverable files**.

2. **Review** the **Lab Assessment Worksheet**. You will find answers to these questions as you proceed through the lab steps.

3. **Review** the Assessing and Auditing an Existing IT Security Policy Framework Definition lab in this lab manual for the policies you aligned to the risks, threats, and vulnerabilities identified in a typical IT infrastructure.

4. In your text document, **list** the gaps you discovered in the Assessing and Auditing an Existing IT Security Policy Framework Definition lab and the policies you suggested.

5. In your Lab Report file, **write** an IT security definition for one of the gaps you have not identified a policy for by suggesting how to mitigate the risk involved. Be sure to **write** a policy statement for this gap that explains how the type of risk should be mitigated. Your policy statement should **outline** the policy itself, any guidelines or standards that should be adhered to in the policy, and any procedures that must be followed when mitigating the risk.

> ▶ **Note:**
> Keep in mind that a policy should be simple, concise, and clearly written. You're writing not only the policy statement, but also the procedural "how-to" to mitigate your chosen type of risk. This is how you would expect to address a newly discovered risk in the real world, at the policy and guideline level.

6. **Review** the following characteristics of the mock XYZ Credit Union/Bank:

   - The organization is a regional XYZ Credit Union/Bank that has multiple branches and locations throughout the region.
   - Online banking and use of the Internet are the bank's strengths, given its limited human resources.
   - The customer service department is the organization's most critical business function/operation.
   - The organization wants to be in compliance with the Gramm-Leach-Bliley Act (GLBA) and IT security best practices regarding its employees.
   - The organization wants to monitor and control use of the Internet by implementing content filtering.

- The organization wants to eliminate personal use of organization-owned IT assets and systems.
- The organization wants to monitor and control use of the e-mail system by implementing e-mail security controls.
- The organization wants to fill the gaps identified in the IT security policy framework definition.

7. Using the following template and the characteristics from the previous step, in your Lab Report file, **create** an organization-wide policy that incorporates the policies you aligned to the risks and the newly written policy definition for one of the gaps:

XYZ Credit Union/Bank

{Insert the Policy Definition Name Here}

Policy Statement

{Insert the policy you wrote for the selected IT security policy definition from step 5.}

Purpose/Objectives

{Insert the policy's purpose as well as its objectives; use a bulleted list of the policy definition. Be sure to explain how this policy definition fills the identified gap in the overall IT security policy framework definition and how it mitigates the risks, threats, and vulnerabilities identified.}

Scope

{Define this policy and its scope and whom it covers.

Which of the seven domains of a typical IT infrastructure are impacted?

What elements, IT assets, or organization-owned assets are within the scope of this policy?}

Standards

{Does this policy point to any hardware, software, or configuration standards?

If so, list them here and explain the relationship of this policy to these standards.}

Procedures

{Explain in this section how you intend on implementing this policy organization-wide.}

Guidelines

> ▶ **Note:**
> Do not forget to also address roles and responsibilities. You will document who would implement the guideline's procedures, and how that person (role) is accountable.

{Explain in this section any roadblocks or implementation issues that you must address and how you will overcome them as per defined policy guidelines.}

> ▶ **Note:**
> This completes the lab. **Close** the **Web browser**, if you have not already done so.

Evaluation Criteria and Rubrics

The following are the evaluation criteria for this lab that students must perform:

1. Define the policy statement for various IT security policy definitions. – **[20%]**
2. Identify key elements of IT security policy definitions as part of a framework definition. – **[20%]**
3. Reference key standards and requirements for IT security policy definitions needed for a framework definition. – **[20%]**
4. Incorporate procedures and guidelines into an IT security policy definition example needed to fill a gap in a framework definition. – **[20%]**
5. Create an IT security policy definition for a risk mitigation solution for an IT security policy framework definition. – **[20%]**

Lab #10 - Assessment Worksheet

Aligning an IT Security Policy Framework to the Seven Domains of a Typical IT Infrastructure

Course Name and Number: _____

Student Name: _____

Instructor Name: _____

Lab Due Date: _____

Overview

In this lab, you defined the policy statement for various IT security policy definitions, you identified the key elements of IT security policy definitions as part of a framework definition, you referenced key standards and requirements for IT security policy definitions, you incorporated procedures and guidelines into an IT security policy definition example needed to fill a gap in a framework definition, and you created an IT security policy definition for a risk mitigation solution for an IT security policy framework definition.

Lab Assessment Questions & Answers

1. Define a policy statement (in two or three sentences maximum) for each of the following policy definitions that are needed to remediate identified gaps for an IT security policy framework:

   - Access control policy definition
   - Business continuity: Business impact analysis (BIA) policy definition
   - Business continuity and disaster recovery policy definition
   - Data classification standard and encryption policy definition
   - Internet ingress/egress traffic and Web content filter policy definition
   - Production data backup policy definition
   - Remote access Virtual Private Network (VPN) policy definition
   - Wide Area Network (WAN) service availability policy definition
   - Internet ingress/egress availability (denial of service/distributed denial of service [DoS/DDoS]) policy definition
   - Wireless Local Area Network (WLAN) access control and authentication policy definition
   - Internet and e-mail acceptable use policy definition
   - Asset protection policy definition
   - Audit and monitoring policy definition
   - Computer security incident response team (CSIRT) policy definition

- Security awareness training policy definition